REVELATIONS:

A

COMPANION

TO THE

"NEW GOSPEL OF PEACE."

ACCORDING TO ABRAHAM.

NEW YORK:
PUBLISHED BY M. DOOLADY, Agent,
49 WALKER STREET.
1863.

REVELATIONS.

CHAPTER I.

1. The Revelation. 2. The War. 3. The Patriarch. 4. The Brigadiers. 5. Shoddee. 8. The Patriarch clothes his Brigadiers. 12. Temple of High Shoddee. 14. The Patriarch's little story.

1. Behold! O my Patriots, the mystery is revealed; even unto babes and sucklings.

2. In the reign of the Patriarch horrid war filled the land with wailing, even the fair land of Jonathan.

3. From morn till night, and from night till morn, there was no rest for the people; for did not the voice of the Patriarch continually cry, "Raze it, raze it; there's nobody hurt, there's nobody hurt."

4. So the Brigadiers went up and down the land, seeking whom they might devour.

5. In that never-to-be-forgotten reign there arose in the city of the Gothamites many who were possessed of a *devil* (the word *devil* means Niggero in the original), who were denominated

in the census of the mighty city, Ripuplicanas, which signifies the followers of Beelzebub, alias Shoddee.

6. And they were not like other men; for they believed *black* was *white*, only a little more so.

7. But they cried unto the Patriarch, and the Patriarch was their friend.

8. Now as the Patriarch grew plucky, he summoned his brave Brigadiers, and answered unto them and said: "Behold! my valiant cocks, your seedy toggery; your shocking bad 'ats; your hungry soles. I, even I, the Patriarch, will cover your nakedness. Ye shall stand adorned with the blue of the skies, and stars shall bedeck your shoulders."

9. When the Patriarch had "dried up," the assembled throng gave him a Tigahah, and went their way rejoicing.

10. Then there was naught heard throughout the land, save the noise of the shearers as they sheared their sheep, and the buzz of the wheels within wheels of the mighty works, until the martial hosts the Patriarch had summoned were equipped as their worshipful lord had commanded.

11. So when all this was accomplished, the Ripuplicanas, the followers of Beelzebub, alias

Shoddee, were full of glee and gold; for did not they *shear* the *sheep;* and did not they move the wheels; and were not they the priests of the new order of Shoddee; and theirs the *blood* of the *prophets?*

12. Then did the Ripuplicanas, followers of Beelzebub, alias Shoddee, wax fat and saucy, and they said one to another, Let us up and build us an altar even in the place of our High Shoddee, called Fifthavynew. There let us build it, and place upon it the figure of our god, even a molten Niggero, and fall down and worship it in the sight of all the people; for we shall thereby find favor with our father the Patriarch.

13. So they straightway went and did according to their counsel. And, behold an altar of brown stone richly carved, and above it the figure of the idol of the great Shoddee, which may be seen there even at this day.

14. And the noise of their rejoicing reached the ears of the Patriarch, and he was exceeding glad. And unto his chief priest and scribe he answered and said, "That reminds me of a little story." Thereupon he related the following narrative: "In the days of the Lawgiver, certain of the people, forgetting that it was because of their observance of the Compact they had been brought in safety out of the land of Egypt, did

with malice prepense gather themselves together unto Abraham, and said, Be thou our ruler. And Abraham "saw it," and did as they desired. Then did the spirit of the Lawgiver cry: "The people have corrupted themselves." But Abraham answered and said, "The Compact is played out. I have put my foot down; and when I raise it again it will be felt in the seat of war."

15. Here the laugh of the Patriarch's chief priest and scribe came in, upon which the Cabinet of the Patriarch was adjourned.

16. Behold! O my patriots, the end of the First Chapter.

CHAPTER II.

1. The Wail. 2. Webfoot. 3. Morgahno. 7. The Gourd Story. 11. The Brigadiers down on Webfoot. They desire a seafaring man. 13. The Cottonade. 14. Loyalty.

1. AFTER these things there came a wail from the great deep; for mighty was the damage the foe had done thereon.

2. Then the Patriarch clapped his hands, and summoned unto his presence his Seacretary called Webfoot, and answered unto him and said. "Buy

me ships wherewith I may float my Brigadiers to the battle-field to crush the Cottonade."

3. And when the Patriarch had ended his speech, his Seacretary Webfoot clapped his hands, and summoned unto his presence his faithful Morgahno, whose name was great "on change," and answered unto him and said, "Buy me ships wherewith I may, or may not, float my brave Brigadiers to the battle-field to crush the Cottonade."

4. So his faithful Morgahno did as he was commanded, and the wail returned to the deep, and many were the ships that the faithful Morgahno bought, so that soon did he jostle the crowd of devotees at the altar of High Shoddee, and great was the stir in their midst as he counted out his gold-offering.

5. Then did the Seacretary Webfoot go straightway into the presence of the Patriarch, and unto his majesty did say: "Look out, O Patriarch, upon the deep, and tell me what thou seest." And the Patriarch rose up and gazed upon the face of the waters, until a mighty storm arose and floated his brave Brigadiers from his sight.

6. And the Patriarch cried with a loud voice unto his chief priest and scribe: "O Seaword! cover me with a gourd."

7. Then unto his Seacretary Webfoot he an-

swered, and said, "That reminds me of a story: There was a certain man named Jonah, who cried unto the people, saying: 'Let them turn every one from his evil way, and from the violence that is in their hands.' They turned; and Jonah was angry." Hence the gourd story.

8. Now, my Webfoot, which of us resembles Jonah the most?

9. Echo answered, Who!

10. So when the Ripuplicanas, followers of Beelzebub, alias Shoddee, heard of all the great things that had been done upon the sea, they were filled with rejoicing, and said: Who so great as the Patriarch; and Webfoot is his prophet.

11. But the brave Brigadiers were down on Webfoot and his faithful Morgahno; and they prayed the Patriarch to grant them another Seacretary, even a sea-faring man.

12. Moreover, notwithstanding, nevertheless, the Patriarch disturbed not his Cabinet furniture; and he did continue to declare to the people the wisdom and greatness of his Seacretary Webfoot.

13. Then did it come to pass that the Ripuplicanas, followers of Beelzebub, alias Shoddee, seeing the mind of the Patriarch, did take and load many ships with merchandise and sail them to

the Cottonade, and there barter the merchandise for the treasure of Niggero, and return with their vessels heavy laden, to bow the knee anew at the shrine of the great Shoddee.

14. And thus did the Ripuplicanas, followers of Beelzebub, alias Shoddee, testify their loyalty to the land of their fathers.

15. And continually did they cry unto the Patriarch, and the Patriarch was their friend.

16. Behold, O my Patriots, the end of the Second Chapter.

CHAPTER III.

1. The War. 2. The needy Brigadiers. 4. The Patriarch's tears. 6. Another story. 13. Achancammerone. 15. The uneasy Brigadiers. 20. The Reason of their Disquiet. 24. The Remedy. 27. The Spoils. 29. The Scribes and Pharisees murmur. 30. They disturb the Patriarch. 41. The cause of their murmurings. 43. The Remedy. 53. Achancammerone goeth abroad. 56. A great Feast.

1. AND the war was grievous in the land.

2. And it came to pass that there was sore need among the hosts of the Patriarch, so that the brave Brigadiers cried aloud unto the Patriarch.

3. O most Lengthy Potentate! didst thou not command the heavens to clothe us, and the

stars to glitter on us? Alas! alas! No sooner was thy command obeyed than our toggery vanished like the baseless fabric of a vision, leaving no rag behind. Be merciful unto thy servants, even as Scotchplaidy was merciful unto thee.

4. And the spirit of the Patriarch was stirred within him. He arose and viewed his brave Brigadiers,—and wept.

5. Then with a loud voice he cried unto them: "This reminds me of a little story."

6. There was a certain king, who had an honest minister.

7. One day the spirit moved the king to command his minister to tell his mind concerning him.

8. Whereupon the minister fell upon his face, and said: O thou Mighty One! thy servant must speak the words of truth and soberness: "Thou art weighed in the balances, and found wanting." "Thy kingdom is divided."

9. And when the Patriarch had made an end of speaking, the multitude shouted: Long live the Patriarch, our Great Potentate!

10. And every man went his way

11. And the Patriarch entered into the Palace of the Whiteman, even into the innermost chamber.

12. There did the Patriarch remain fasting

many days and nights, until the shadow of the Patriarch had nearly disappeared.

13. Then summoned he unto him his familiar, yclept Achancammerone, surnamed Bellicose,

14. And thus did he discourse:

15. I pray thee tell me, my familiar, why all this disquiet among my brave Brigadiers?

16. Why do they rage, and imagine a vain thing?

17. Whereupon, Achancammerone, the Patriarch's familiar, surnamed Bellicose, answered him, and said:

18. It becometh not thy servant, O, thou Wisest of Mortals, to show thee what thou already seest.

19. Rather let me be numbered with those who have merited thy displeasure.

20. But, O Patriarch, I make me bold to say, thy brave Brigadiers imagine *not* a vain thing. They rage; but there is method in their raging.

21. The Patriarch bade his familiar speak on.

22. Now know, Most Elevated One, that the children of this world are wise in their generation. Therefore do I declare unto thee my whole counsel.

23. The Patriarch bade his familiar speak on.

24. Give thou, O Dispenser of Patronage,

unto these men to plume themselves with the spoils, as becometh the victors to do. Bid them feather their nests with the fat things which are the pride of the foe. Say unto them: Gather the gold and precious stones, and bedeck ye yourselves and your wives, your children and servants; and clothe ye your households in fine linen, even in the royal purple.

25. Speak thus unto them, O thou Most Honest Ruler, and as thy servant liveth, thou shalt no more be vexed.

26. And the Patriarch said—nary a word.

27. However, there was great spoil taken; of gold, and silver, and precious stones; linen and royal purple; and great was the prey that was taken, both of man and of beast.

28. And great was the rejoicing of the people; and gayly did the brave Brigadiers drive their fast horses in the broad ways before the temple of High Shoddee.

29. But certain of the scribes and pharisees, who dwelt in the city of the temple of High Shoddee, murmured against the Patriarch's familiar, Achancammerone, surnamed Bellicose.

30. And the noise of their murmurings reached the ears of the Patriarch.

31. So it came to pass that the Patriarch hid himself as before in his most secret chamber.

32. And, after much fasting, he clapped his hands, and summoned again unto him

33. Achancammerone, his familiar, surnamed Bellicose.

34. And thus did he discourse.

35. I pray thee, my familiar, tell me why the money-changers quarrel in the place of High Shoddee?

36. Why do the scribes write bitter things against their ruler?

37. Why do the pharisees put on airs?

38. And the Patriarch's familiar answered him and said:

39. Behold, O Sagacious Sage, as thy servant liveth I will speak the truth.

40. The Patriarch bade his familiar speak on.

41. Do thou, O Warrior of the Whitehouse, bid them gather weapons of war for thy brave Brigadiers.

42. Do thou bid them lay up of the treasure which thou controllest.

43. Do thou create new posts of honor for them, which shall fill them to repletion with the great mammon.

44. And as thy servant liveth, they shall no longer vex thee, O most Amiable Sovereign.

45. And the Patriarch was—mum.

46. Then there arose a great shout in the palace of High Shoddee.

47. And the scribes sang the praises of the Patriarch throughout the length and breadth of the land.

48. The pharisees forgot the Samaritans in their glee.

49. And all the people united in the shout: Long live the Patriarch, and Achancammerone his *prophet!*

50. So the fame of Achancammerone spread abroad; and he was known far and near.

51. Thereupon the Patriarch bethought him to send his familiar, Achancammerone, surnamed Bellicose, to foreign lands; that the name and fame of the Patriarch might be known throughout the earth.

52. For the Patriarch was ambitious.

53. So the Patriarch sent his familiar to a far distant country, to tell the heathen of the great Patriarch who ruled the western hemisphere.

54. And the Patriarch saw what he had done, and was satisfied.

55. But his familiar, Achancammerone, surnamed Bellicose, said—nary a word.

56. Then there was a great feast in the place of the High Shoddee; and the air rang with the

shouts of the multitude; and the great idol Niggero glittered and glistened in the sun:

57. For the scribes and pharisees were as an army with banners.

58. And the people cried unto the Patriarch, and the Patriarch was their friend.

59. Behold, O my Patriots, the end of the Third Chapter.

CHAPTER IV.

1. Horace the Grilleyte and Henry the Raymite. 5. "I am here." 7. Herod-bar-Stantine. 8. The Acts of Achancammerone. 9. His record.

1. In those days there were two scribes, one Horace the Grilleyte and Henry the Raymite, who gave the Patriarch no peace, neither day nor night.

2. Then was the Patriarch greatly troubled. And hid himself from the sight of men for many days.

3. And it came to pass that the Patriarch opened his mouth and said:

4. Oh that my familiar, even Achancammerone, surnamed Bellicose, were not in my thoughts.

5. Then, as it were in the twinkling of an eye,

he heard the voice of his familiar saying, "I am here."

6. So Horace the Grilleyte and Henry the Raymite gave the Patriarch no peace, neither day nor night.

7. And the Patriarch's familiar was thrust from his presence, and Herod-bar-Stantine was chosen from among the people to minister unto the Patriarch in his stead, for did he not out-Herod Herod.

8. Thus endeth this record of the deeds of Achancammerone, surnamed Bellicose.

9. But are not his mighty acts written in the pages of the archives in the temple of Beelzebub in the palace of the High Shoddee!

10. Behold, O my Patriots, the end of the Fourth Chapter.

CHAPTER V.

1. Chason the Treasurer. 2. His skill in Metallurgy and Astrology. 3. Star-gazing. 4. He soliloquizes. 7. A graven image, and what he will do with it. 12. A No. 1. 14. The Patriarch's disturbers.

1. Now there was one of those who stood in high places before the Patriarch, who was called Chason the Treasurer, whose duty it was

to look after the Patriarch's money-bags in the fair land of Jonathan.

2. This Chason the Treasurer was skilled in metallurgy and astrology. And daily did he study the one, and nightly did he delight in the other.

3. So it came to pass one night, as he sat gazing at the stars, that a lucky thought struck him, and thus did he soliloquize:

4. "Am I not A No. 1? Do I not rule on change and control the sinews of war? Am I not alone worthy to receive the mantle of the Patriarch?

5. O Stars! how shall I obtain the prize?

6. Ah! I have it!

7. I will make unto myself a graven image of my patron Beelzebub, alias Shoddee, and this will I imprint in living green on fairest linen bands.

8. And on the face thereof will I put the likeness of Chason the Treasurer, the successor of the Patriarch.

9. These linen bands will I scatter broadcast among the people. Then will the Patriarch be forgotten, and Chason the Treasurer be remembered in the land forevermore."

10. And straightway went Chason the Treasurer, and did as he had devised.

11. And he scattered the fair linen bands with

backs of living green up and down the highways, so that there was no man to be found in the land that had not one of the fair linen bands.

12. Then Chason the Treasurer stood A No. 1 before the people.

13. But the Patriarch was from that day no longer before the people as A No. 1.

14. And Horace the Grilleyte and Henry the Raymite gave the Patriarch no peace neither day nor night.

15. Behold, O my Patriots, the end of the Fifth Chapter.

CHAPTER VI.

1. Confiscation. 4. Bootyler. 5. Bearfremount. 6. The Wailing of the Women and Children. 8. Bootyler's Deeds. 12. Bearfremount's Ambition. 13. The Patriarch's Indignation. 17. The Perseverance of the Patriarch's Messengers. 21. The Patriarch's latest Joke.

1. Now it came to pass that certain leaders of the brave Brigadiers, who had buckled on their armor at the eleventh hour, because of the tidings of the great spoil their brethren had taken from the foe, did beseech the Patriarch to declare unto the people the statute known as "Confiscation."

2. For, said they, if thou doest but this, O most Illustrious Ruler, thy brave Brigadiers shall be as the sands of the sea for multitude, and *we*, most noble Patriarch, will lead them on to victory.

3. And in an evil hour the Patriarch raised his foot.

4. So the brave Brigadiers returned to the war: and they were led in the way of the Cottonade by him whom the Patriarch called Bootyler;

5. And in the way of the Niggero by him whom the Patriarch called Bearfremount.

6. And great was the wailing of the women and children at the Cottonade.

7. And the spoil of Bootyler was more than the ships of the Patriarch could transport.

8. And his deeds, if they should be all written, I suppose that even the temple of High Shoddee itself could not contain the books that should be written.

9. But Bearfremount looked not alone to spoil, for was he not lord of Mariposa?

10. Therefore did he seek occasion to gain the favor of the false god, Niggero, that he might betray the Patriarch into the hands of the Philistines.

11. So he bade his heralds declare to the

people wheresoever he tarried, the new dispensation of which he was the sole originator and dispenser.

12. And he did establish his court, and issue his decrees, as though the Patriarch had deceased and was gathered to his fathers.

13. But a bird did carry the news to the house of the Whiteman, and to the ear of the Patriarch; and he became exceeding wroth, even foaming at the mouth in his great indignation.

14. For the Patriarch read the thought that was in the breast of Bearfremount, as though Bearfremount had said: Oh that I were made judge in the land, that every man which hath any suit or cause might come unto me, and I would do him justice!

15. So the Patriarch dispatched his messengers to bid Bearfremount to come unto him.

16. But sorely vexed were the Patriarch's messengers.

17. Yet did they persevere, until, by wonderful strategy, they placed the Patriarch's command before the dread Bearfremount.

18. Then did the tidings of their success thrill the heart of the Patriarch, like as it were the tidings of a great victory.

19. So when Bearfremount was come unto

the house of the Whiteman, the Patriarch rushed forth, and fell upon his neck and embraced him, saying, Never more, my beloved Bearfremount, shalt thou hazard thy life for *my* sake; sit thou here at my right hand.

20. And there was great rejoicing throughout the land.

21. And the meeting of the Patriarch and Bearfremount was recorded in the pages of Seaword's book as "the Patriarch's latest joke."

22. Behold, O my Patriots, the end of the Sixth Chapter.

CHAPTER VII.

1. The Spoil. 2. Contention. 5. The Captives. 7. Emancipation. 8. The Patriarch a Planter. 10. Another Story.

1. AND the spoil, both of men and beasts, was very great.

2. So that there was much contention touching the division thereof.

3. And the noise of the contentious ones ascended to the ear of the Patriarch.

4. And he said unto the contentious ones, Why quarrel ye concerning the captives, even in the face of the foe?

5. And they answered him, and said, It is for the *good* of the captives we do this thing.

6. But the Patriarch read their thoughts afar off.

7. Therefore did he declare unto the people a new statute, called "Emancipation," which caused all such spoil to fall to the share of the Patriarch.

8. For, behold! my people, said the Patriarch, I will take possession of the fairest lands of the foe, and I will cause these my captives to till the soil thereof, and great shall be the gain to the Patriarch.

9. And the Patriarch was well pleased with "Emancipation."

10. Then said the Patriarch to the assembled multitude, That reminds me of a story:

11. A certain man named Abram went up out of Egypt, he, and his wife, and all that he had, and Lot with him, into the south.

12. And Abram was very rich in cattle, in silver and in gold.

13. And he went on his journeys from the south even to Bethel, unto the place where his tent had been at the beginning, between Bethel and Hai;

14. Unto the place of the altar, which he had made there at the first: and there Abram called on the name of the Lord.

15. And Lot also, which went with Abram, had flocks, and herds, and tents.

16. And the land was not able to bear them, that they might dwell together: for their substance was great, so that they could not dwell together.

17. And there was a strife between the herdmen of Abram's cattle and the herdmen of Lot's cattle: and the Canaanite and the Perizzite dwelt then in the land.

18. And Abram said unto Lot, Let there be no strife, I pray thee, between me and thee, and between my herdmen and thy herdmen; for we be brethren.

19. Is not the whole land before thee? Separate thyself, I pray thee, from me: if thou wilt take the left hand, then I will go to the right; or if thou depart to the right hand, then I will go to the left.

20. And Lot lifted up his eyes, and beheld all the plains of Jordan, that it was well watered everywhere, before the Lord destroyed Sodom and Gomorrah, even as the garden of the Lord, like the land of Egypt, as thou comest unto Zoar.

21. Then Lot chose him all the plain of Jordan; and Lot journeyed east: and they separated themselves the one from the other.

22. And when the Patriarch had made an end

of speaking, the assembled multitude sent up a shout in praise of the Patriarch, for the Patriarch was their friend.

23. And Horace the Grilleyte and Henry the Raymite were among the multitude, and they remembered the Patriarch's story.

24. Behold, O my patriots, the end of the Seventh Chapter.

CHAPTER VIII.

1. The War. 4. The Patriarch's Speech. 18. And there was a Pause. 20. The only Speaker left.

1. Yet did the war desolate the land, and the prophets saw no signs of peace.

2. So the Patriarch summoned all the wise men of the land to the house of the Whiteman, that they might take counsel together concerning the war.

3. And when they were assembled in the presence of the Patriarch, he spoke unto them, saying,

4. Ye men of the fair land of Jonathan, I appear before you on this august occasion that I may see you and be seen by you. Although I summoned you hither, it was but for this great purpose—to see and be seen.

5. And that I might call your attention, in particular and public manner, to the only clause of the Compact that I decreed should be permitted to stand.

6. O ye men of the fair land of Jonathan, have you forgotten that these immortal words were the first your Patriarch uttered in your ears?

7. Have you forgotten how often your Patriarch has since their first utterance repeated them to you?

8. And now I again say that the great privilege you enjoy as my subjects, and the only one left you from the Compact, is—*to see and be seen!* (Sensation.)

9. Oh that you would live up to the spirit of these words.

10. If you would but see and be seen there would be an end to war.

11. If you would but see and be seen, I could bid adieu to my body-guard.

12. If you would but see and be seen, I could remain your Patriarch, and live and die seeing and being seen.

13. But ye are a stiff-necked and perverse people, therefore have I caused a new statute to be promulgated, to be called the "Expatriation," which my brave Burnsydy will declare unto you.

14. So that hereafter, ye men of the fair land of Jonathan, do ye naught else, but *see and be seen.*

15. Then did the wise men depart in silence,

16. And no one durst speak; for, to be loyal, he must only see and be seen.

17. And it came to pass that silence brooded over the once fair land of Jonathan; and there was no sound heard throughout the length and breadth thereof save the clicking of the instruments called Telegraphs, which carried the Patriarch's immortal proclamation—*See and be seen*—from pole to pole.

18. In the place of the High Shoddee not a word was heard; and men bowed the knee in silence.

19. By the river of Patome the brave Brigadiers saw, and were seen by the foe; and all was quiet there.

20. Now there was but one speaker left in the land, and he, the Patriarch.

21. Behold, O my Patriots, the end of the Eighth Chapter.

CHAPTER IX.

1. Silence. 2. The Patriarch reasons. 6. The Patriarch reads. 34. The Patriarch muses. 37. The Patriarch soliloquizes. 41. The Patriarch's Policy. 43. The Patriarch's Preachers.

1. AND it came to pass that while silence reigned in the fair land of Jonathan, the Patriarch bethought him of the saying,—Wisdom is better than strength.

2. And thus to himself he spake: What hindereth now?

3. Yea, I will search the books of the wise and holy of the earth, that peradventure I may find therein written the thing I desire to know, even the way of deliverance for my people.

4. And he straightway sought far and near in the fair land of Jonathan, and he found the books he desired.

5. Then sat he himself down in the innermost chamber of the house of the Whiteman;

6. And he gave himself no rest neither day nor night, that he might find the precious words.

7. And Horace the Grilleyte and Henry the Raymite were filled with confusion.

8. Then the Patriarch opened a book, and with a loud voice did he utter:

9. "The words of wise men are heard in quiet

more than the cry of him that ruleth among fools."

10. The Patriarch turned on.

11. "There is an evil which I have seen under the sun, as an error which proceedeth from the ruler."

12. The Patriarch closed that book, and opened another.

13. "Christianity quite annihilates the disposition for martial glory."

14. "To sacrifice our lives for the liberties, and laws, and religion of our native land, are undoubtedly high-sounding words:—but who are they that will do it? Who is it that will sacrifice his life for his country? Will the senator who supports a war? Will the writer who declaims upon patriotism? Will the minister of religion who recommends the sacrifice? Take away glory—take away *war*, and there is not a man of them who will do it."

15. The Patriarch threw that book down in disgust, and opened another.

16. "You would, perhaps, die to *save* your country; but this is not the question. A soldier's death does not save his country. The question is, whether, without any of the circumstances of war, without any of its glory or its pomp, you are willing to resign yourself to the

executioner. If you are not, you are not willing to die for your country."

17. The Patriarch mused a moment, then turned on.

18. "Christianity does not encourage *particular* patriotism, in opposition to general benignity."

19. "As long as mankind shall continue to bestow more liberal applause on their destroyers than on their benefactors, the thirst of military glory will be the vice of the most exalted characters."

20. "The safety of nations is not to be sought in arts or in arms. War reverses, with respect to its objects, all the rules of morality. It is nothing less than a temporary repeal of all the principles of virtue. It is a system, out of which almost all the virtues are excluded, and in which nearly all the vices are incorporated. In instructing us to consider a portion of our fellow-creatures as the proper objects of enmity, it removes, as far as they are concerned, the basis of all society, of all civilization, and virtue; for the basis of these is the good will due to every individual of the species."

21. The Patriarch shook his head, and turned on.

22. "There is but one community of Christians in the world, and that, unhappily, of all communities one of the smallest, enlightened

enough to understand the prohibition of war by our Divine Master, in its plain, literal, and undeniable sense; and conscientious enough to obey it, subduing the very instinct of nature to obedience."

23. The Patriarch grew red in the face, slung the book behind him, and opened another.

24. "They who defend war, must defend the dispositions which lead to war."

25. The Patriarch adjusted his spectacles, read the passage again, and—turned on.

26. "I am persuaded that when the spirit of Christianity shall exert its proper influence over the minds of individuals, and especially over the minds of public men in their public capacities, over the minds of men constituting the councils of princes, from whence are the issues of peace and war—when this happy period shall arrive, war will cease throughout the whole Christian world."

27. "Morality and religion forbid war in its motives, conduct, and consequences."

28. The Patriarch's countenance assumed a grave cast. He laid the book carefully down, and took up another.

29. "Be at peace among yourselves. See that none render evil for evil to *any man.* God hath called us to peace."

30. "*Avenge* not yourselves. If thine enemy hunger, feed him; if he thirst, give him drink. Recompense to *no man* evil for evil. Overcome evil with good."

31. "It has been said, Thou shalt not kill, and whosoever shall kill, shall be in danger of the judgment; but I say whosoever is *angry* with his brother without a cause, shall be in danger of the judgment."

32. The Patriarch was disturbed.

33. "All they that take the sword shall perish with the sword."

34. The Patriarch could read no farther; but fell back upon his couch in a deep and painful revery.

35. For a long time he remained silent.

36. Then he arose, and paced the chamber with a firm step, and an air of resolution.

37. And thus did he soliloquize:

38. If these things that I have read be true; if it be true that there is a "*new commandment*" which is to be obeyed instead of "an eye for an eye, a tooth for a tooth," then I must at last adopt a—Policy. What shall it be?

39. At that moment the Patriarch's eye fell upon a page of the book as it lay open before him, and read these words:

40. "The Preacher sought to find out accept-

able words: and that which was written was upright, even words of truth."

41. Ah! happy thought, the Patriarch cried, I have found a policy.

42. And thus did he reason within himself.

43. Are not my preachers called to declare the things I this day have read? Is it not their mission to proclaim "peace on earth, and good will to men?" Is it not their duty to tell the people of the "*new commandment?*"

44. This very day (the Patriarch continued) will I publish my Policy; and it shall be known in the land as—"The Conscription."

45. Behold! O my Patriots, the end of the Ninth Chapter.

CHAPTER X.

1. The Summons. 3. The Patriarch's Speech. 12. The People rejoice. 16. The Patriarch's Wisdom. 18. Conscription. 22. The Beecherite. 24. The Cheeverite. 26. Philip the Amalgamator. 30. "I will be the Leader." 31. The Patriarch's Satisfaction. 32. The Great Commission. 33. The End not Yet.

1. THEN it came to pass that the Patriarch did summon every man throughout the length and breadth of the land to the Palace of the Whiteman.

2. And when the people had assembled themselves before the Patriarch, thus did he address them:

3. Ye men of the western hemisphere, give ear unto your Patriarch.

4. Your Patriarch is well pleased with your obedience to his mandate,—*See and be seen.*

5. He is well pleased with your obedience to it, that he has directed this mandate to continue in force until the end of the war. (Applause.)

6. Your Patriarch summoned you here to-day in order that he might say this to you; and that he might see you, and be seen by you on this glorious occasion.

7. He has also something new to make known unto you,—he has a Policy. (Sensation.)

8. This policy is called, "The Conscription." (Breathless silence.)

9. The Patriarch thus understands this Policy. The brave Brigadiers are to be called back from the Cottonade, and their places are to be supplied from the ranks of the clergy!

10. Thus will the Patriarch place his preachers where they may give practical effect to their teachings; and to their labors does the Patriarch look for the return of *blessed peace.*

11. (The Patriarch here became too much af

fected to prolong his remarks, and the multitude returned to their respective abodes.)

12. And there was great rejoicing among the people, because the preachers were chosen to go against their enemies; For, said every man, are they not called to proclaim "the glad tidings of salvation, and to publish Peace!"

13. Blessed peace-makers!

14. They shall deliver our unhappy land from the scourge of the sword.

15. Then did all the people speak one with another of the great things the preachers should do.

16. And greatly did they magnify the wisdom of the Patriarch, saying, Behold a wiser than Solomon.

17. But the preachers were—mum

18. And the Patriarch caused the preachers to be gathered together according to the Conscription.

19. And when they were assembled without the camp, the Patriarch with his body-guard, and the chiefs among his brave Brigadiers, went forth to meet them.

20. And when the Patriarch drew near, every man of them was debating with his fellow touching the war, and great was the confusion of their tongues, for as yet they had no leader.

21. So it came to pass that, when the Patri-

arch saw they had no leader, he waxed exceeding wroth.

22. And the Patriarch said unto them, Where is he who did so loudly proclaim the Gospel of Sharp's Rifles? He, even the Beecherite shall lead you.

23. But the Beecherite could not be found, for aforetime had he taken counsel with himself, and said: "I will get me to the far distant Angle-land, and there will I tarry till this cruel war is over."

24. And the Patriarch said unto them, Where is he who calleth Niggero his better? He, even the Cheeverite shall lead you.

25. But the Cheeverite could not be found, for he had fled for safety to the temple of the Woolly-heads.

26. And the Patriarch said unto them, Where is Philip the Amalgamator? He shall lead you.

27. And some answered him, and said, Behold, O Patriarch, we have sent messengers unto Philip, the Amalgamator, to bid him be one with us, but he hath replied, Your banner is not my banner, therefore will I not go.

28. And other some answered him, and said, We pray thee, O Patriarch, to be charitable unto Philip, the Amalgamator, for perchance he may have taken him a wife from among the

daughters of Niggero, and therefore he cannot come.

29. Then did the Patriarch again address them, saying, Tell me which one from among you shall be your leader.

30. And the assembled preachers, as with the voice of one man, each for himself, did cry, I will be the leader.

31. And the Patriarch saw what was in their mind, and he was satisfied.

32. So he commanded them to go forth upon their mission, taking naught with them but their Great Commission.

33. *And the end was not yet come.*

www.ingramcontent.com/pod-product-compliance
Lightning Source LLC
LaVergne TN
LVHW011123110826
845150LV00008B/2230

* 9 7 8 1 4 1 8 1 9 5 2 0 5 *